HURRICANE
IRMA

BY EDWARD WILLETT

CONTENT CONSULTANT

JENNIFER COLLINS
ASSOCIATE PROFESSOR, SCHOOL OF GEOSCIENCES
UNIVERSITY OF SOUTH FLORIDA

Essential Library

An Imprint of Abdo Publishing | abdopublishing.com

abdopublishing.com

Published by Abdo Publishing, a division of ABDO, PO Box 398166, Minneapolis,
Minnesota 55439. Copyright © 2019 by Abdo Consulting Group, Inc. International
copyrights reserved in all countries. No part of this book may be reproduced in
any form without written permission from the publisher. Essential Library™ is a
trademark and logo of Abdo Publishing.

Printed in the United States of America, North Mankato, Minnesota
012018
012018

Cover Photo: Gary Lloyd McCullough/The Florida Times-Union/AP Images
Interior Photos: Jose Jimenez Tirado/Getty Images News/Getty Images, 4–5, 8,
40–41; Orien Harvey/Lonely Planet Images/Getty Images, 10–11; Spencer Sutton/
Science Source, 12; Red Line Editorial, 16, 26; Lt. Cmdr. Nathan Hann/NOAA, 21; Jiri
Vondrous/Shutterstock Images, 22–23; R. Nicolas-Nelson/French Defence Ministry/
AP Images, 28; Mark Wilson/Getty Images News/Getty Images, 32–33; Alan Diaz/
AP Images, 36, 54–55; Bill White/NASA, 38; Valentine Autruffe/AFP/Getty Images,
45; Tatiana Fernandez/AP Images, 49; Ramon Espinosa/AP Images, 53; Mike
Stocker/South Florida Sun-Sentinel/AP Images, 58; Ethan Daniels/Shutterstock
Images, 65; Stephen B. Morton/AP Images, 66–67; Mic Smith/AP Images, 69; Mass
Communication Specialist 3rd Class Kaitlyn E. Eads/US Navy, 72–73; Christophe
Ena/AP Images, 75; Salwan Georges/The Washington Post/Getty Images, 78; MOD/
AP Images, 80; Desmond Boylan/AP Images, 82; Al Diaz/Miami Herald/AP Images,
84; Andy Newman/AP Images, 90–91; NOAA/AP Images, 95; Drew McArthur/
Shutterstock Images, 99

Editor: Arnold Ringstad
Series Designer: Maggie Villaume

Publisher's Cataloging-in-Publication Data

Names: Willett, Edward, author.
Title: Hurricane Irma / by Edward Willett.
Description: Minneapolis, Minnesota : Abdo Publishing, 2018. | Series: Special reports
Identifiers: LCCN 2017956009 | ISBN 9781532114014 (lib.bdg.) | ISBN 9781532152917
        (ebook)
Subjects: LCSH: Natural disasters--Juvenile literature. | Hurricanes--Juvenile
        literature. | Disaster relief--Juvenile literature. | Gulf Coast (U.S.)--
        Juvenile literature.
Classification: DDC 976.044--dc23
LC record available at https://lccn.loc.gov/2017956009

CONTENTS

CHAPTER ONE

A TASTE OF
THINGS TO
COME

Elessa Harris, 22, thought she knew hurricanes. She lived on the small Caribbean island of Barbuda, and hurricanes are a fact of life in that part of the world. On September 5, 2017, as Hurricane Irma approached, she took shelter in her house like she had before. She waited to ride out the storm.

Harris soon discovered Hurricane Irma was different. The wind blew faster and faster. Eventually it started lifting the roof right off her house. Panicked, she ran to a neighbor's home and hunkered down there for the rest of the storm. When she and her neighbors emerged the next day, they found their entire town

Aerial photos revealed the scope of Irma's destruction in Barbuda.

had been destroyed. "I have witnessed hurricanes before," Harris said, "but nothing like this."[1]

Weather authorities had been tracking Irma for days. With winds reaching 185 miles per hour (296 kmh), it was one of the most powerful hurricanes ever recorded in the Atlantic. Barbuda was the first inhabited area the storm struck.

CATASTROPHIC DAMAGE

By the time Irma had moved on from Barbuda, there was little left standing on the once-pristine island. The winds had snapped the island's only communications tower in half, so telephone service was out. As a result, it took hours for news from the island to reach the outside world. When it did, it became clear the devastation was almost total.

WHAT IS A HURRICANE?

A hurricane is a rotating low-pressure weather system with wind speeds at or exceeding 74 miles per hour (119 kmh). The term *hurricane* comes from Hurakan, the Mayan god of wind and storms. Hurricanes originate in the Atlantic basin, which includes the Atlantic Ocean, the Caribbean Sea, and the Gulf of Mexico. The time of year in which most hurricanes occur is known as hurricane season. It officially lasts from June 1 to November 30, though hurricanes can also form outside of this time frame. The season peaks between August and October. On average, there are 12 hurricanes per year in the Atlantic basin.[2] Hurricanes also occur in other ocean basins. In some parts of the world they have regionally specific names. In the Northwest Pacific they are called typhoons. But in the eastern North Pacific they are called hurricanes.

Roderick Faustin, an official with Barbuda's government, told the *Los Angeles Times* on September 7 that at least 95 percent of the properties on the 62-square-mile (160 sq km) island were either damaged or totally destroyed.[3] That included the schools, the only hospital, the airport, and two hotels.

NO ONE LEFT

Although humanitarian aid began to arrive on the island immediately after the storm, the destruction was so complete that the government decided to evacuate the entire remaining population. In total, 1,700 people were taken from Barbuda to Antigua. A state of emergency was declared. "For the first time in 300 years, there is not a single living person on the island of Barbuda," Ronald Sanders, the Antigua and Barbuda

BARBUDA

Barbuda is part of the Leeward Islands chain in the eastern Caribbean. It's located approximately 260 miles (420 km) southeast of Puerto Rico and 110 miles (180 km) north of Guadeloupe. A coral island famous for its white-sand beaches, Barbuda rises to only 144 feet (44 m) at its highest point. Along with the larger island of Antigua, located 39 miles (62 km) to the south, Barbuda is part of the nation of Antigua and Barbuda. The country's population is more than 90,000.[4] Most of those people live on Antigua. Prior to Hurricane Irma, Barbuda was home to approximately 1,700 people.

Many residents of Barbuda took shelter in a sports stadium on Antigua.

ambassador to the United States, told Public Radio International.[5]

IRMA'S FIRST CASUALTY

One death was reported on Barbuda. Carl Junior Francis, a two-year-old toddler, was ripped from the arms of his caregiver by the wind. That caregiver told Eli Fuller, a volunteer from Antigua delivering supplies, that as the roof came off and the walls caved in, she had one arm around a post in her house and the other arm around the child.

"The wind just pulled the child out of her hands and that was the last they saw of the child," Fuller told the *New York Post*. "And then they found the child the next morning dead."[6] Francis had been the first fatality from Irma. He would not be the last.

A PATHWAY OF DESTRUCTION

Irma left a trail of devastation as it moved across the Caribbean and the southeastern United States. It finally dissipated on September 16, 11 days after it struck Barbuda. It killed at least 130 people.[7] The total damages rose into the tens of billions of dollars.

Hurricane Irma was a powerful reminder of the destructive power of nature and the vulnerability of human settlements on islands and in coastal regions. The storm also raised questions about the future. How did global climate change contribute to its strength? And how could people in the path of future hurricanes better prepare for storms of this magnitude?

"I WOULD HAVE CRIED BECAUSE THAT DEVASTATION WAS SO HEART WRENCHING. I COULDN'T BELIEVE IT. IT'S ONE OF THE WORST FEELINGS I'VE EVER FELT IN MY ENTIRE LIFE."[8]

— GASTON BROWNE, PRIME MINISTER OF ANTIGUA AND BARBUDA

CHAPTER TWO

A HURRICANE
IS BORN

O n August 27, 2017, a weak wave of low pressure in the atmosphere left the western African coast, accompanied by showers and thunderstorms as it moved into the Atlantic Ocean. Just nine days later, it would slam into Barbuda as a devastating hurricane. While the strength of Hurricane Irma was unusual, the way it formed was not.

Weather disturbances like the one that became Hurricane Irma move off the African coast every few days during hurricane season. Most of them fail to develop any further. They may be disrupted by arid winds coming from the Sahara Desert, or they may be torn apart by strong, high-altitude air currents blowing from west to east.

Stormy weather in the ocean off the coast of Africa eventually morphed into a deadly hurricane thousands of miles to the west.

For a hurricane to develop from one of these low-pressure waves, it needs several things. One of the most important is warm ocean water, at least 80 degrees Fahrenheit (27°C). That's because above all else, a hurricane needs energy, and warmer water provides more of it than colder water.

The first step in a hurricane's formation is the familiar water cycle. Water at the surface of the ocean evaporates, rises, forms clouds, condenses, and falls as rain, creating thunderstorms. Some areas have conditions that lead them to develop more thunderstorms than others. As a

Hurricanes result from and are sustained by the complex interaction of warm and cool air in the atmosphere.

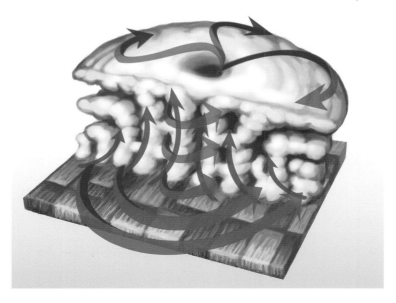

result, the air in those areas contains more water vapor. That water vapor traps the heat from the warm ocean water, causing even more evaporation and a general upsurge of warm air.

As that air rises, other air rushes in to take its place. The newly arriving air becomes warm and humid, rises to form more clouds, and generates more rain. This creates a self-reinforcing cycle. As thunderstorm activity continues to grow, a disturbance forms. If this disturbance begins to spin around a closed center, it becomes a tropical depression. This spin happens because as the Earth rotates, it drags the atmosphere along with it. However, this rotation is fastest at the equator, so the air closer to the equator moves faster than the air farther from the equator. This phenomenon is called the Coriolis effect. Storms north of the equator spin counterclockwise, while storms south of the equator spin clockwise.

When the winds in the system reach or exceed 39 miles per hour (63 kmh), it is called a tropical storm and is given a name. When the storm intensifies further, reaching 74 miles per hour (119 kmh), it becomes a hurricane. An area known as the eye forms in the center. This is where the air pressure is lowest. Despite the winds swirling all around it, the eye is very calm and clear.

IRMA INTENSIFIES

By the morning of August 30, the storm's average wind speed had risen above 39 miles per hour (63 kmh). This elevated it to the status of a tropical storm. It was also given its name at this point. Irma continued to intensify, and within 30 hours its average wind speeds were reaching 115 miles per hour (184 kmh). This made it a Category 3 hurricane. To meteorologists, hurricanes at this category or higher are known as major hurricanes. Irma's rapid increase in strength was the first sign the storm would be something special. It's unusual for storms in the far-eastern Atlantic to intensify that quickly.

HOW ARE HURRICANES NAMED?

Hurricanes are given names to make it easier to identify them in communications and forecasts. Names also help avoid confusion when there are two or more storms occurring at the same time. Hurricanes in the Caribbean were once named after the saint's day on which they occurred. For example, Hurricane Santa Ana devastated Puerto Rico on July 26, 1825, the feast day of Saint Anne. An Australian meteorologist, Clement Wragge, began giving women's names to tropical storms in the late 1800s. The United States began using women's names for hurricanes in 1953. In 1978, it began using both men's and women's names, alternating with each storm.

Over the next few days, Irma moved through a region with drier air at high altitudes. Its strength remained steady. However, on September 4 and 5, as it approached Barbuda, it encountered warmer water and a moister atmosphere. As a result, it intensified rapidly once again, becoming the Category 5 monster that hit Barbuda. Irma remained a Category 5 hurricane for three days, making it the first recorded storm to do so since satellites were first used to study hurricanes.

On September 8, Irma weakened slightly, though as a Category 4 storm, it remained incredibly strong. It moved through the southern

HURRICANE CATEGORIES

Hurricanes are categorized based on their sustained wind speed using the Saffir-Simpson Hurricane Wind Scale, which ranges from Category 1 to Category 5. Sustained wind speeds indicate how much damage a hurricane may cause. Category 1 hurricanes have winds between 74 and 95 miles per hour (119–153 kmh). These storms can damage trees and roofs, and they can knock down power lines. Category 2 hurricanes have winds between 96 and 110 miles per hour (154–177 kmh). They cause more severe destruction, uprooting trees and heavily damaging roofs. Category 3 hurricanes have winds between 111 and 129 miles per hour (178–208 kmh). Damage from these storms is devastating, and the infrastructure for delivering electricity and water may be knocked out for days or weeks. Category 4 hurricanes have winds between 130 and 156 miles per hour (209–251 kmh). They can blow the roofs off buildings and snap trees in half. The most powerful hurricanes are Category 5 storms. Their sustained winds exceed 157 miles per hour (252 kmh). They destroy a high percentage of houses and infrastructure in the area, leaving a region virtually uninhabitable.

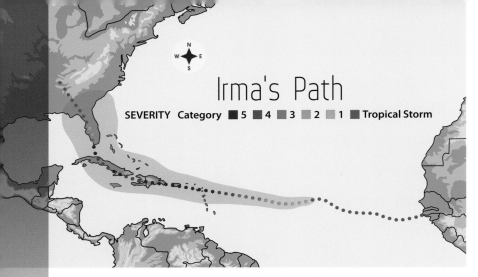

Hurricane Irma picked up strength as it moved west across the Atlantic Ocean toward the Caribbean.

Bahamas, then strengthened again to Category 5 that evening as it returned to open water and approached the coast of Cuba. The storm weakened again as it skimmed along the Cuban coastline. Interaction with land disrupts hurricanes because they require a lot of deep, warm water right underneath their centers in order to maintain the extremely low pressure that generates their strong winds. In addition, hurricanes lose energy to friction as their winds hit land, and high-altitude land formations disrupt the storms' circulation. Irma left Cuba as a Category 3 hurricane.

TURNING NORTH

Up until then, Irma had been steered westward by a strong high-pressure region of the atmosphere.

That high-pressure ridge began to break down on September 9, allowing Irma to turn to the northwest, toward the Florida Straits. It intensified yet again, returning to Category 4, as it approached the Florida Keys and made landfall at Cudjoe Key on September 10. However, it was beginning to encounter unfavorable atmospheric conditions. When it made landfall in mainland Florida, near Marco Island later that day, it was a Category 3 storm again.

DEATH OF A HURRICANE

Irma weakened as it moved inland. By the afternoon of September 11, Irma was in southern Georgia. Its winds had slowed enough to downgrade it to a tropical storm. By that evening, as it continued north across central Georgia, it was downgraded further, to a tropical depression.

The remnants of Irma continued moving over a wide swath of the US Midwest and East Coast. Satellite imagery on September 13 showed clouds stretching from Missouri to the southern tip of the Great Lakes. The clouds moved northeast the next day across Pennsylvania and New York, before finally sliding off into the Atlantic on September 15.

HURRICANE FORECASTING

Once a hurricane has formed, scientists can predict its track, or path, three to five days into the future. That possible trajectory is represented as a widening cone, because the uncertainty increases the further the forecast is extended. Predictions as to how intense a hurricane will become are even more uncertain because the processes by which hurricanes intensify are very complex and still not fully understood.

In the United States, hurricane forecasts are made by the National Hurricane Center. The forecasting process begins with observations, not only from satellites but also from aircraft, ships, buoys, radar, and land-based stations. While the hurricane is over the open ocean, satellites are the primary tool. Using satellite data, forecasters can estimate the location of the storm's center, its motion over the past six to twelve hours, and its maximum wind speed.

If a hurricane poses a threat to the land, aircraft from the US Air Force and the National Oceanic and Atmospheric Administration (NOAA) will fly out to observe the storm directly and take measurements, which are then used to refine the forecasts. Once a hurricane approaches within 280 miles (450 km) of land, ground-based radars provide more precise precipitation and wind velocity data. And once the hurricane actually hits land, automated weather observation stations and weather balloons can provide even more measurements.

All these data are fed into computer programs that use the information to predict the hurricane's track and intensity. A variety of hurricane prediction programs exist, and they all model the atmosphere in different ways. As a result, they can produce very different forecasts. Four times a day, human forecasters sift through the results before issuing a final forecast based on their experience with the different models and the specific characteristics of the storm.

FROM THE
HEADLINES

FLYING INTO THE EYE

One of the critical elements in hurricane forecasts is data from inside the storm. This information can't be obtained from satellites. The only way to get it is to gather measurements right in the heart of the storm itself. "Only if you go into the hurricane can you really get an accurate measure of its exact center location, the structure, the maximum winds," hurricane expert Rick Knabb told the Reuters news agency as Irma approached.[2]

To get those data, pilots from the US Air Force Reserve's 53rd Weather Reconnaissance Squadron in Biloxi, Mississippi—commonly called the Hurricane Hunters—fly a four-engine turboprop aircraft directly into the eye of even the strongest hurricane. The crew drops sensors that transmit data as they fall through the storm. They send back information on pressure, wind speed, and direction. On each mission, the aircraft makes multiple passes into the eye. Crews from NOAA, flying out of Lakeland, Florida, also fly into hurricanes for research purposes.

Despite the turbulence encountered before the planes reach the smooth air in the storm's eye, the last time an aircraft was lost was in 1974. The last close call was in Hurricane Hugo in 1989, when a pilot from NOAA flew in much too low in a storm

Aircraft that fly into hurricanes are packed with sensors, computers, and other equipment.

that was believed to be weaker than it really was. Slammed by higher-than-expected winds, the plane lost an engine, the pilot lost control, and the aircraft descended rapidly. Fortunately, the pilot regained control as the plane entered the eye.

CHAPTER THREE

GETTING READY
IN THE
CARIBBEAN

An early hint of trouble appeared in Hurricane Irma Advisory Number 10, issued by the US National Hurricane Center at 5:00 p.m. Atlantic Standard Time (AST) on Friday, September 1. Although the advisory noted that "there are no coastal watches or warnings in effect," it also said that "interests in the northern Leeward Islands should monitor the progress of this system."[1]

At 11:00 a.m. AST on September 3, Advisory Number 17 added, "Hurricane and Tropical Storm Watches will likely be required for portions of these islands later today or tonight."[2] Hurricane watches followed at

The Caribbean's many small islands, with their populations concentrated along coastal areas, are particularly vulnerable to hurricanes.

5:00 p.m. that afternoon, and the first hurricane warnings were issued for the Leeward Islands at 11:00 a.m. the next day. People and governments in the threatened islands did what they could to prepare. On September 4, the governor of Puerto Rico, Ricardo Rosselló, declared a state of emergency. On September 5, US President Donald Trump declared emergencies in Florida, Puerto Rico, and the US Virgin Islands.

WHAT IS A STATE OF EMERGENCY?

Although the details vary from place to place, in general, when a government declares a state of emergency, this allows it to legally take actions it might not be able to in ordinary times. In the United States, for example, when a state declares a state of emergency, it activates disaster response plans and systems, gives the state authority to spend money on personnel, equipment, and supplies, extends legal protection to people responding to the disaster, and suspends various rules and regulations that might otherwise slow down the response.

A federal declaration of emergency activates federal assistance to states, triggers various emergency provisions in a number of laws, provides additional legal protection, eases additional regulatory requirements, and activates various national response systems. Although a state of emergency is often declared after a disaster occurs, when a disaster can be predicted ahead of time, as in the case of an approaching hurricane, it is often declared in advance to help the country be better prepared.

PREPARING IN PUERTO RICO

Just a few weeks earlier, Hurricane Harvey had produced devastating flooding in Texas and Louisiana. The resources of the Federal Emergency Management Agency (FEMA), the US government agency responsible for responding to disasters, were stretched thin. Still, FEMA began making preparations for the arrival of Irma. Approximately 124 FEMA staff were deployed to the US Virgin Islands and Puerto Rico. Meals and water were prepared on delivery trucks, ready to be driven into disaster areas.

Many other preparations were made by the US federal government and its agencies. The Environmental Protection Agency put out messages about ways to prepare, and it worked to secure hazardous waste sites. The Department of Energy sent responders along with FEMA personnel to help restore power. The National Guard deployed teams to offer support for communications, medical, and security needs. The National Park Service secured its sites and anticipated sending a crew into the US Virgin Islands to help clear roads. The US Geological Survey installed flood sensors in potentially affected areas.

Puerto Rican officials also began evacuations of at-risk areas, and they urged people to prepare for the storm. Although the path of the hurricane was expected to take it north of Puerto Rico, there was concern the island's aging power infrastructure would suffer from the storm's outer edges, with massive power outages possible, along with life-threatening storm surges, rains, and mudslides.

ANTIGUA AND BARBUDA

Antigua and Barbuda would be the first to feel the hurricane's impact. On Barbuda, officials from the Barbuda Council, the police and fire departments, the hospital, and humanitarian organization the Red Cross met to prepare for the impending storm. A team was placed on standby to assist the elderly and disabled and transport them to one of three prepared shelters.

On September 5, Prime Minister Gaston Browne assured residents that relief efforts would begin immediately after the storm, noting there were two

The Caribbean Islands

Tampa · — Orlando

ATLANTIC OCEAN

NASSAU
Miami ■
THE BAHAMAS
HAVANA
TURKS AND CAICOS
DOMINICAN
CUBA
REPUBLIC
BRITISH VIRGIN ISLANDS
HAITI
STO. DOMINGO
US VIRGIN ISLANDS
PUERTO RICO
ANGUILLA
JAMAICA
ST. MARTIN
BARBUDA
KINGSTON
PORT-AU-PRINCE
ST. BARTHÉLEMY
ANTIGUA
ST. KITTS
GUADELOUPE
AND NEVIS
CARIBBEAN SEA
DOMINICA
MARTINIQUE
ST. LUCIA
BARBADOS

military cargo planes on standby in Venezuela and two others being loaded in Miami, Florida. A 20-foot (6 m) container of supplies was packed on Antigua to take to Barbuda as soon as possible after the hurricane, and requests for assistance were sent out around the world, as far away as the Middle East.

GUADELOUPE, SAINT BARTHÉLEMY, SAINT MARTIN

On the French islands of Guadeloupe and Saint Barthélemy and on the French and Dutch island of Saint Martin, schools were closed, and many people were evacuated to shelters. In Guadeloupe, evacuees included not only those on the lower coasts but also those who lived on the edges of seaside cliffs. Officials feared erosion of the cliffs could lead to collapses. Hospitals stockpiled drugs, food, and drinking water, and they checked their generators. The French military sent troops and supplies.

On Saint Barthélemy, home to 11,000 people, local official Anne Laubies told people it was important that they headed immediately for safe locations, noting that the islands had become much more urbanized than when

The French military prepared cargo planes and helicopters to provide relief to the areas in the path of the storm.

the last major hurricane hit 20 years before. Emergency medical teams were also staged on Saint Martin in preparation for the storm's arrival.

TURKS AND CAICOS

In the Turks and Caicos islands, low-lying areas were likewise evacuated, schools closed, and government facilities secured and boarded up. Warnings and instructions on how to prepare for the storm's arrival were sent out in English, Creole, and Spanish through websites, radio broadcasts, text messaging, and social media apps.

Like many of her counterparts around the Caribbean, Dr. Virginia Clerveaux, director of the Department of

Disaster Management and Emergencies for the Turks and Caicos, expressed optimism. "It's a lack of preparedness by residents and other entities that make [hurricanes] a disaster," she said at a press conference on September 4. "We don't expect to have a disaster on our hands because we're expecting residents to play their part."[3]

BAHAMAS

Preparations in the Bahamas included unprecedented emergency evacuations by air of several of the southernmost islands in the chain. It was the largest evacuation in the history of the country. In announcing the effort, Prime Minister Dr. Hubert Minnis cautioned that anyone who remained behind would be risking their lives, and that emergency assistance would be unavailable for an unknown amount of time after the storm passed. In the end, approximately 1,000 people were evacuated. At least 300 elected to remain behind, despite the warning.[4]

HISPANIOLA

The island of Hispaniola is divided into two countries: the Dominican Republic in the east and Haiti in the west.

In the Dominican Republic, preparations included evacuating some 11,200 residents from vulnerable areas.[5]

In addition, 7,400 tourists were moved from beachside hotels to inland areas of the capital, Santo Domingo.[6]

The approach of Hurricane Irma posed greater problems for the impoverished nation of Haiti. There, the government of Prime Minister Jack Guy Lafontant reported that it had sent containers of food to the five regions of the country most likely to be affected, along with bulldozers and earth-moving equipment to open blocked roads. However, after the storm, several mayors of cities in those areas contradicted those claims. They said they had seen no equipment. They said they had to draw on their own limited funds to stock the shelters to which vulnerable residents were evacuated.

"PEOPLE WHO ARE POTENTIALLY IN THE PATH OF A HURRICANE REALLY NEED TO PAY ATTENTION. IF YOU'RE TOLD TO GET OUT, GET OUT—DON'T MESS AROUND."[7]

— KERRY EMANUEL, ATMOSPHERIC SCIENTIST, MASSACHUSETTS INSTITUTE OF TECHNOLOGY

CUBA

In Cuba, the National Civil Defense Council declared a state of alarm for the vulnerable provinces. Local civil defense councils prepared evacuation shelters, laying in stocks of food and water. In Las Tunas province, four short tons (3.6 metric tons) of crackers were stockpiled, and sugar supplies were transported to a safer location so they wouldn't be damaged by the storm.[8] Following carefully drawn-up plans, Cubans collected garbage, cleaned sewers and drainage systems, and secured elevated water tanks.

As the storm approached, the government cut off electricity and gas in an effort to prevent fires and other damage. This left residents without lights, fans, or ways to cook food. Since most people there don't own vehicles, residents were dependent on government trucks and buses to evacuate them. Just as in the Dominican Republic, thousands of tourists were also evacuated.

The Caribbean had done what it could to get ready for Hurricane Irma's arrival. And north of Cuba, the state of Florida was doing the same. The region braced for devastation as Irma continued its march across the Atlantic Ocean.

CHAPTER FOUR

PREPARATIONS IN FLORIDA

O n September 4, when the forecast cone made it clear Irma would impact Florida, Governor Rick Scott declared a state of emergency for all of Florida's 67 counties.[1] Among other things, that declaration allowed him to immediately activate Florida's National Guard to help with preparations and relief operations. By the next day, 4,000 National Guard troops had been activated. Another 3,000 were ordered to report for duty by Friday, September 8.[2]

President Donald Trump followed that on September 5, declaring a prelandfall state of emergency in Florida. That declaration authorized FEMA to coordinate all disaster-relief efforts. That same day, in preparation for evacuations, Governor Scott

Ahead of Irma's landfall, Florida governor Rick Scott urged citizens to heed the warnings of the weather authorities.

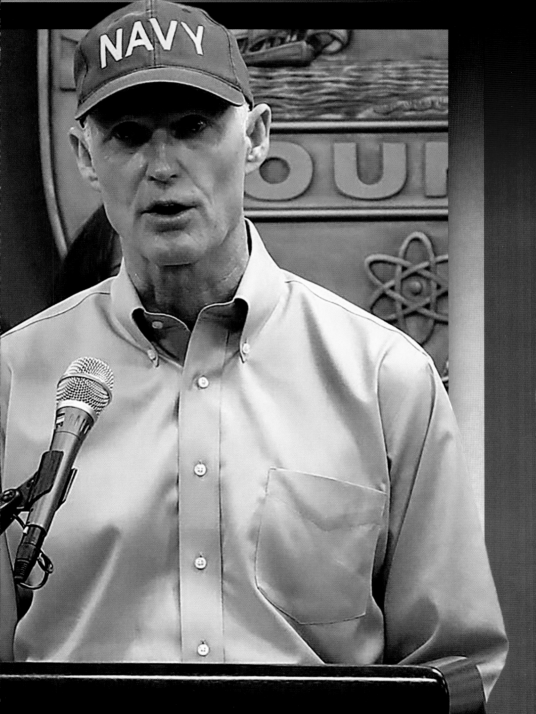

suspended tolls on all of Florida's toll roads as of 5:00 p.m.

By September 9, nearly 7 million people had been told to

evacuate in Florida, Georgia, and South Carolina.[3] Governor Scott warned that all 20 million residents of Florida might be asked to evacuate, pointing

out that Hurricane Irma was wider than the entire state and thus could cause major, life-threatening impacts from coast to coast.

Monroe County, which includes the Florida Keys, announced a mandatory evacuation for all 30,000 residents on September 6.[4] Tourists were to leave that day, and residents the next. As with other places in the hurricane's path, not everyone complied. Miami began ordering evacuations in vulnerable areas, such as Miami Beach, that same day. Residents of Miami-Dade County choosing to stay in their own homes were urged to have at least three days of food and water on hand.

FUEL SCARCE, TRAFFIC SLOW

The scale of the evacuations meant the government's top priority was fuel availability, because gas stations in the evacuation zones were running low. Residents lined up for hours to fuel their vehicles at those stations that remained open. Approximately 300,000 barrels of fuel were delivered by ship to Tampa.[6] A fuel tanker ship from Mississippi was heading to Tampa as well, Governor Scott reported on September 8.

For many drivers, traffic along evacuation routes was backed up and moving very slowly. Linda Caldwell of Daytona Beach told the *New York Times* that she and her family had left at 4:00 a.m. and that it had taken them 12 hours to travel 259 miles (416 km) to Ridgeland, South Carolina, on the way to their final destination of Roanoke, Virginia. "As far as we've gone, it's been bumper to bumper," she said.[7]

In an effort to reduce some of the congestion, the Florida Department of Transportation authorized vehicles to use the shoulder lanes on Interstate 75 for a roughly 150-mile (240 km) stretch between Wildwood, Florida,

and the Georgia state line. However, it didn't allow the use of the southbound lanes for northbound traffic because they were needed for emergency vehicles and critical shipments of gasoline and other supplies to South Florida.

Airports and airlines were similarly jammed. Airport parking garages in Miami, Orlando, and Fort Lauderdale were full. By midday on September 8, at least 875 arriving and departing flights had been canceled at those airports.[8] By late afternoon on September 10, the airports had ceased operations entirely. Cruise ships were affected, too, with numerous cruises canceled, rescheduled, or rerouted.

Several Orlando theme parks, including Walt Disney World, closed in anticipation of the storm. It was the fifth time since 1971 that the famous park had been closed because of a storm, and the second year in a row. It had closed in October 2016 when Hurricane Matthew threatened. Since Walt Disney World generates about $30 million of revenue a day, the shutdown was expensive.

KENNEDY SPACE CENTER CLOSES

Kennedy Space Center, where the US space agency NASA launches many of its rockets, also closed in preparation for

Many Floridians fled north as the storm approached.

A small group of people known as the rideout team stayed behind at Kennedy Space Center when Irma hit.

the storm. The private rocket company SpaceX managed to launch one of its Falcon 9 rockets just in time, firing the rocket into orbit at 10:00 a.m. on September 7 as workers rushed to prepare for the coming hurricane. If the launch had been delayed, the rocket would have had to have been hauled back into a hangar to ride out Irma.

A team of approximately 140 people were left at the space center as the storm closed in, tasked with monitoring critical equipment and infrastructure. Merritt Island, where the space center is located, was one of the areas covered by a mandatory evacuation order.

GEORGIA AND OTHER STATES

Many of the preparations made in Florida were echoed farther north. Georgia governor Nathan Deal declared a state of emergency for all six coastal counties in the state on September 6, and he expanded it to cover 30 counties in southeast and east central Georgia on September 7. On September 8, he expanded the state of emergency to cover 94 counties south of the Atlanta metropolitan area.[9] Finally, on September 10, the state of emergency was extended over the entire state. Atlanta, for the first time ever, was placed under a tropical storm warning.

States of emergency were also declared in North Carolina by Governor Roy Cooper and in South Carolina by Governor Henry McMaster. The governor of Virginia, Terry McAuliffe, followed on September 8, not only to protect his own residents, but also to allow him to mobilize resources to support his neighboring states.

The scale of preparations was enormous in both the Caribbean and in the United States. But no one could know for certain if they were enough. These areas and the world waited to see what would happen when Hurricane Irma finally made landfall.

CHAPTER FIVE

IRMA HITS
THE ISLANDS

I n pitch-black darkness at 2:00 a.m. on Wednesday, September 5, Hurricane Irma howled ashore on Barbuda. Maurice George, a visual arts teacher at Barbuda's secondary school, had stayed on the island, taking shelter at his father's house. As the storm hit, the wind and rain threatened to rip off the roof over his head.

When the brief calm in the eye of the storm passed over, George and his father fled the crumbling building. "But the hurricane came back while we were on the road," he told a British newspaper. "We had to dodge wires and lamp posts to get to my cousin's house."[1]

After the storm passed, Antigua and Barbuda prime minister Gaston Browne flew above the island.

The hurricane's brutal winds ripped apart structures on Barbuda, severely damaging nearly every building on the island.

He described the damage as "like having a bomb literally thrown on a city." The wind was so strong, he said, it fired "missiles" of debris at residents and structures.[2]

An estimated 95 percent of the buildings on the island suffered at least some damage. Many lost their roofs; others were completely destroyed. Parts of the island were underwater. The island was essentially uninhabitable. Just how strong the winds were when Irma hit Barbuda couldn't be said with certainty. One anemometer, a device for measuring wind speed, registered a gust of 155 mph (254 kmh) before suddenly falling to zero, an indication it had been ripped away by the wind.[3]

It was a devastating enough storm that it was surprising that only one person was killed, two-year-old Carl Junior Francis. Barbuda was fortunate in that the larger, neighboring island

DEATH OF A SURFER

Although Hurricane Irma passed well south of Barbados as it hit the Leeward Islands, it claimed one of its first victims there. Zander Venezia, a 16-year-old professional surfer, was surfing the giant waves generated by the approaching storm at a beach called Box by Box, famous for its high waves during storms. A particularly vicious wave slammed him into a reef, where he hit his head. Knocked unconscious, he drowned. Venezia, whose father was also a surfer, had been surfing since he was five years old. He was considered a contender to be on the Barbados Olympic team in 2020, when surfing was slated to make its debut as an Olympic sport.

of Antigua, a 90-minute boat ride away, escaped relatively unscathed, although there was some roof damage, flooding, and downed trees. That gave the people of Barbuda somewhere to go when it became clear they couldn't remain on their own island.

SAINT MARTIN, SAINT BARTHÉLEMY, AND ANGUILLA

Just six hours after striking Barbuda, Hurricane Irma's eyewall made landfall on Saint Martin. Only 12 miles (19 km) long from north to south, and about the same distance wide, the island is split into French and Dutch halves. It's home to more than 70,000 people.[4] Irma damaged or destroyed at least 70 percent of the infrastructure on the island.[5] Daniel Gibbs, president of the French territory, told reporters, "There are shipwrecks everywhere, destroyed houses everywhere, torn-off roofs everywhere."[6] Things were no better on the Dutch side. "It's like someone with a lawn mower from the sky has gone

"IT'S AN ENORMOUS CATASTROPHE. NINETY-FIVE PERCENT OF THE ISLAND IS DESTROYED. I'M IN SHOCK. IT'S FRIGHTENING."[7]

— DANIEL GIBBS, PRESIDENT OF THE TERRITORIAL COUNCIL, SAINT MARTIN over the island," said Mairlou Rohan, a visiting European tourist.[8]

The death toll was much higher there than in Barbuda. A total of fourteen people were killed, ten on the French side and four on the Dutch side, and more than 100 people were injured. Approximately 2,800 tourists were caught in the storm, some of them capturing footage from their hotel balconies showing submerged cars and ruined buildings far below.

On the Dutch side, the Princess Juliana International Airport, famous worldwide because planes landing there fly low over the heads of the tourists on a popular beach, suffered severe damage. Boarding walkways were tossed around, planes were damaged by flying rocks, and huge mounds of sand blocked the runway.

Saint Barthélemy was similarly devastated. During the storm, a reporter in a hotel that was supposed to be safe found that several rooms had simply been destroyed. The concrete walls vibrated like cardboard. Other survivors said that when the storm had passed, it looked like a bomb had exploded and burned all the vegetation. Roofs were gone, and trees were downed. The surging ocean had taken

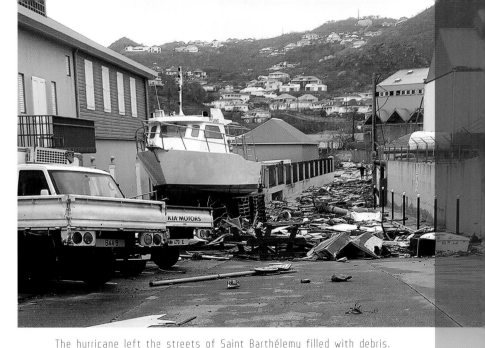

The hurricane left the streets of Saint Barthélemy filled with debris.

everything out of the houses and flooded the streets and the airport. On both islands, residents were left without water, electricity, or phone service.

As the eye of the storm passed over Saint Martin, the northern eyewall passed over Anguilla, a 35-square-mile (91 sq km) island about 12 miles (19 km) to the north. Another popular tourist spot, Anguilla has a population of about 17,000. The storm hit the island hard. One person was killed, and approximately 70 percent of the island's critical infrastructure was destroyed, cutting off water and electricity.[9] The island's police and fire stations, hospitals, and schools, as well as a senior citizens' home, were all damaged or destroyed. A lawyer on the island,

Josephine Gumbs-Connor, said Irma left the island in "absolute pieces," adding, "When you look at our island at the moment you would think that it just suffered nuclear bomb devastation."[10]

THE VIRGIN ISLANDS

At about 2:00 p.m. on Thursday, September 6, the core of Irma passed over the northernmost Virgin Islands. This collection of 90 small islands is located about 50 miles (80 km) east of Puerto Rico. The chain stretches about 60 miles (96 km) west to east, and it is split between the British Virgin Islands and the US Virgin Islands.

The British Virgin Islands consist of four large islands (Tortola, Anegada, Virgin Gorda, and Jost Van Dyke) and 32 smaller ones. More than 20 of these are uninhabited. They lie north and east of the US islands, which consist of three large islands (Saint Croix, Saint John, and Saint Thomas) and approximately 50 smaller ones. Approximately 35,000 people live in the British Virgin Islands, and 107,000 live in the US Virgin Islands.

All the Virgin Islands suffered severe damage. Five people were killed in the British Virgin Islands, and four in the US Virgin Islands. In the British Virgin Islands, Governor Gus Jaspert declared a state of emergency, the first ever for the territory. Among the many buildings destroyed was the National Emergency Operations Center. As on all the islands, trees were down, roads were blocked, power and water were knocked out, and debris was scattered everywhere.

Kennedy Banda, a resident of Tortola in the British Virgin Islands, told news network CNN that he and his wife, four children, and mother-in-law left their house to shelter in a hotel. They barricaded themselves in the room and used mattresses and chairs to block the glass door. "I went back to the house and the fridge was in the water," he said. "Our beds, the clothes, everything was blown out."[11] On Saint John, there were harrowing accounts of people's houses flying away while they were in them.

PUERTO RICO

Hurricane Irma's eye missed Puerto Rico, passing just north of the island at about 8:00 p.m.

"WE DESPERATELY NEED HELP AS SOON AS POSSIBLE. FOOD, WATER, SHELTER. I'M EXTREMELY CONCERNED ABOUT HEALTH AND SAFETY—THERE IS SEWAGE ABSOLUTELY EVERYWHERE."[12]

— NATALIE DRURY, RESIDENT OF TORTOLA

on September 6. It was still classified as a Category 5 storm. Although Puerto Rico avoided a direct hit, waves of up to 30 feet (9 m) were reported. Governor Ricardo Rosselló declared a state of emergency for the hardest-hit area, the islands of Culebra and Vieques to the east.[13]

Four deaths were attributed to the storm. One man fell off his ladder while repairing his roof. Another was struck by lightning. A woman fell from a wheelchair while being evacuated and hit her head, and another person died in a car accident caused by the weather. Even without a direct hit from the storm, more than 100 homes were destroyed, trees were downed, and 70 percent of the population of 3.3 million was left without power.[14] Tens of thousands were left without fresh water. Puerto Rico had dodged the worst of Irma, but just weeks later it would be devastated by Hurricane Maria. Maria further damaged the island's infrastructure, heavily affecting an area already reeling from an economic crisis.

HISPANIOLA

The next morning, September 7, at about 4:00 a.m., Irma passed north of Hispaniola. Though spared a direct hit, the Dominican Republic suffered considerable damage, including flattened buildings, downed trees and power lines, and storm surges. The storm also destroyed a bridge over the Massacre River, which linked the town of Dajabon in the Dominican Republic with Ouanaminthe in Haiti. More than 5,000 people had been evacuated as the hurricane approached.[15]

In Haiti, the damage to farmers was severe. Just 11 months earlier, Haiti had suffered a direct hit from

In the Dominican Republic, electric company workers quickly cleared dangerous debris that brought down power lines.

Hurricane Matthew, which made landfall on the country's southern tip, wiping out farms and livestock with heavy rains and winds reaching 145 miles per hour (232 kmh). The hurricane killed 546 people. Farmers struggling to reestablish their crops, including bananas, avocados, yams, and breadfruit, were hit again by Irma.

TURKS AND CAICOS ISLANDS

At about 7:30 p.m. on September 7, Hurricane Irma reached the Turks and Caicos Islands, two groups of islands on the southeastern edge of the Bahamas, north of Hispaniola. There are eight large coral islands and numerous smaller ones. The Turks group is composed of Grand Turk Island, Salt Cay, and several lesser islands. The Caicos group is northwest of the Turks. Most of the population of about 30,000 lives on Grand Turk in the Turks group and on two islands in the Caicos Group, South Caicos and Providenciales.

Irma's eye passed over South Caicos. The storm's most powerful winds, blowing at 175 miles per hour (280 kmh), raked the islands to the north for more than two hours. Grand Turk Island took the brunt of the storm. Roofs were ripped off, streets flooded, and power and water were lost. The hospital in the capital, Cockburn Town, was also damaged, but no deaths were reported.

THE BAHAMAS

Early the next morning, Saturday, September 8, Irma's eye passed over the southern Bahamas. Now a Category 4 storm, it still brought winds of 155 miles per hour (248 kmh) as it scored a direct hit on

Duncan Town. The only settlement on tiny Ragged Island was home to 72 people. Irma destroyed every home, the health facility, and the school, and it knocked out power and water service.[16] All inhabitants were subsequently evacuated, and the island was declared uninhabitable.

Elsewhere in the Bahamas, homes were damaged and power lines downed, but no casualties or damage to infrastructure were reported. Although spared the hurricane itself, the northern Bahamas suffered damage from tornadoes spawned by the storm. Multiple homes lost their roofs on Grand Bahama.

CUBA

Irma intensified after it left the Bahamas, becoming a Category 5 storm again. At 11:00 p.m. it made landfall in Cuba, on the Camagüey Archipelago. It was the first Category 5 hurricane to hit Cuba in 85 years.

The storm tore through the central and western provinces of the island nation, causing catastrophic destruction and killing at least ten people. At least five of those deaths were caused by the collapse of the country's ramshackle old buildings, many of which had not been well maintained. The official state-run newspaper, *Granma*, estimated that just in Havana, at least 157 homes were destroyed and an additional 4,288 weakened by wind, rain, and flooding.[18] The country's electrical grid was badly damaged too, and the damage to the island's banana, rice, and sugar crops was described as "incalculable" by officials.[19]

Among the hardest-hit places was the region surrounding the town of Caibarién, popular with tourists.

By dawn on Saturday, September 9, waves were rolling down the town's main street. Within hours, Caibarién was under several feet of water. The damage continued along the coast as Irma advanced, with waves 16 to 23 feet (5 to 7 m) tall recorded in some places.[20] By late morning, Irma had weakened to a Category 3 storm, losing energy as it clawed across the Cuban landscape. Still, it continued to cause significant damage until, late in the day, it finally left the island and headed toward its next target: Florida.

Irma brought massive storm surges to the streets of downtown Havana, Cuba.

CHAPTER SIX

LANDFALL
IN FLORIDA

Hurricane Irma officially made landfall in the United States at Cudjoe Key, one of the Florida Keys, at 9:10 a.m. on Sunday, September 10. It remained a Category 4 storm, with peak winds of 130 miles per hour (208 kmh). Following Hurricane Harvey's landfall in Texas just 16 days earlier, it marked the first time in recorded history that two Category 4 hurricanes made landfall in the contiguous United States in the same year.

Although Cudjoe Key was the first place struck, all the islands of the Florida Keys were affected, with a quarter of the homes destroyed and 65 percent of them suffering major damage. Winds overturned and ripped open homes, damaged docks, uprooted trees,

The Keys, the first part of Florida to be hit, suffered severe damage from Irma's winds and flooding.

and tossed boats around. Power, water, and cell phone service were all disrupted. Some towns were completely drowned by the storm surge. "Everything is underwater, I mean everything," said Larry Kahn, a local newspaper editor, describing the town of Marathon.[1] The Keys' 70,000 residents had been ordered to evacuate, but an estimated 10,000 stayed.[2]

George Ramos, who lives on Summerland Key, was one of those who stayed. He told the *New York Post* that the sea poured into his garage, leaving fish in his swimming pool and a boat in his back garden. "The storm sounded like war," he said. "It sounded like explosives."[3]

RARE DEER SPARED

Irma threatened an entire species' survival when it hit the Florida Keys. The National Key Deer Refuge is home to the tiny Key deer, only 30 inches (76 cm) tall. The deer are found there and nowhere else on Earth. But the deer proved resilient. A total of 949 survived the storm in good shape. Only 21 were killed by the storm itself.[4]

SECOND LANDFALL

After leaving the Keys, Irma took aim at the mainland. It made its second landfall at Marco Island in southwestern Florida at 3:35 p.m. as a Category 3 storm. Its sustained winds blew at 115 miles per hour (184 kmh), with gusts peaking at 130 miles per hour (208 kmh). Though still a major hurricane, it was far less powerful than the Category 5 monster that had rampaged across the Caribbean starting with the destruction of Barbuda. There was a general sense that things could have been a lot worse if it had made landfall farther to the east or if it had not weakened during its time over Cuba. If those things had happened, Miami could have been catastrophically flooded. More than 80 percent of Miami-Dade County is no more than 10 feet (3 m) above sea level.[5] Instead, the only reported flooding in Miami was on Brickell Avenue in the city's financial district. This area is near Biscayne Bay, where water rose several feet up staircases and storefronts.

Even in the west, things could have been worse. A research model had suggested Naples could receive a storm surge of more than 10 feet (3 m). Instead, the waters crested at about half that height. Another potentially vulnerable city was Tampa, Florida. A storm surge of just 17 feet (5 m) could put most of the city underwater.[6]

A STROKE OF LUCK

What made the difference was a little bit of good luck.

If Irma had stayed off Florida's Gulf Coast, the eastern

eyewall's strong winds could have shoved more water

into Fort Myers and Naples and swamped Tampa Bay

and Saint Petersburg. But Irma

veered inland just before it got

to Naples, pulling the eastern

wall away from the ocean.

The winds on the north side

of the storm were blowing

west and actually pulled

"WHEN THE SUN CAME UP, IT WAS A GOOD DAY. BECAUSE CONSIDERING WHAT WE WERE FACING, THIS COULD HAVE BEEN A VASTLY DIFFERENT SCENARIO."[7]

— BOB BUCKHORN, MAYOR OF TAMPA

water away from the shore. In Tampa, for example, water

levels dropped five feet (1.5 m), baring the ocean floor

a considerable distance to sea. In Sarasota, observers

saw this phenomenon strand a manatee on the shallow

coastal floor.

Once the eye of the hurricane passed, the back

side of the storm, whose winds blew to the east, pulled

the water back to the coast. But by this time, the storm

had weakened, so the resulting surge wasn't as strong

Some Miami streets suffered from significant flooding.

as expected. Rather than nine feet (3 m) of water in neighborhoods in East Naples, for example, only about a foot (0.3 m) showed up. Some parts of Tampa and Saint Petersburg experienced two to three feet (0.6 to 1 m) of storm surge.

Evidence of the weakening was seen in Fort Myers. The center of the storm passed over the city at about 7:15 p.m., but rather than being a well-formed eye, it was full of jumbled, thinner clouds. This was a sign that the spinning structure of the hurricane had begun to fail.

The fact that Miami, on the east coast of Florida, experienced any flooding at all was due to the immense size of the storm, which covered the state from coast to coast, allowing the hurricane's wind to push water ashore on both sides. The worst flooding actually occurred farther north. Although downgraded to a tropical storm as it moved north, Irma created seven feet (2.1 m) of storm surge in some areas. The city of Jacksonville, in northeastern Florida, declared a flash flood emergency on Monday, September 11, due to a combination of storm surges and the flooding Saint Johns River. At 2:00 p.m. Monday, at high tide, a gauge showed the river at three feet (1 m) above flood stage, the height at which a river begins to threaten the nearby area. This was a record for the city, eclipsing one set during Hurricane Dora in 1964 by at least one foot (0.3 m).[8]

DEVASTATING WIND DAMAGE

Julie Halley, who rode out the storm with her children and extended family in her house in Saint Petersburg, described what it was like. "My heart just pounded in my chest the whole time," she told CNBC. "You hear stuff hitting your roof. It honestly sounds like somebody is just whistling at your window the whole night. It's really scary."[9]

"WE WERE LYING ON THE FLOOR OF THE CLOSET, TAKING SHELTER DURING ONE OF THE TORNADO ALERTS DURING THE NIGHT, AND WE WERE BOTH CRYING."[10]

— JORGE MEDINA, RESIDENT OF FORT LAUDERDALE

Parts of two construction cranes collapsed in Miami, and another collapsed in Fort Lauderdale, despite being engineered to withstand winds of 145 miles per hour (232 kmh). There was no way to move the massive cranes before the hurricane arrived. The counterbalance can weigh 30,000 pounds (13,600 kg), as much as ten small cars. Miami officials said it could take two weeks to move them, and hurricanes don't give that much warning.

Strong winds kept officials from responding at first, which left the cranes' arms where they had fallen, high atop buildings. Fortunately, no injuries were reported in any of the collapses. It could have been much worse, with more cranes potentially collapsing had Irma scored a direct hit on eastern Florida. Again, there was a feeling of relief. Miami resident Marco Hildago told the *Miami Herald*, "Thank God Irma didn't come. It would have erased us off the map."[11]

FALL OF THE MOON TREE

One casualty of Hurricane Irma was a historic sycamore tree at Kennedy Space Center known as a Moon Tree. During the Apollo 14 moon landing mission in 1971, astronaut Stuart Roosa carried hundreds of tree seeds in small canisters aboard the spacecraft. After the astronauts' safe return, the seeds were distributed to dozens of locations across the United States. One went to Kennedy Space Center. Though it had survived a journey to the moon and back, the center's Moon Tree was no match for Hurricane Irma's winds.

THE DEATH TOLL MOUNTS

The fact Irma could have been worse was of little consolation to those who lost friends and loved ones to the storm. By early October, the official death toll from Irma in the state of Florida stood at 66. However, that figure did not include a dozen people, aged 57 to 99, who died in hot, humid conditions after a nursing home in Broward County lost its air-conditioning for three weeks post-Irma.

Of the deaths attributed to the storm, twenty were caused by blunt-force injury or some kind of impact, which indicates they were killed in traffic crashes, hit by flying debris, or trapped in collapsing structures. Eight people drowned. Thirteen died from carbon monoxide poisoning, often caused by running gas-powered generators indoors without sufficient ventilation.[12] Other causes of death included heat exhaustion and health issues, such as heart attacks and complications related to diabetes.

By the time it left Florida, Irma was no longer a hurricane. Downgraded to a tropical storm, it headed next into Georgia. Hurricane or not, its journey of destruction was still not over.

FROM THE
HEADLINES

HOW HURRICANES
AFFECT MARINE LIFE

Hurricanes damage more than just trees, roads, and buildings. They can also have a devastating impact on marine life in the shallow waters close to affected islands. The winds and storm surges can rip both plant and animal life from the seafloor, leaving behind only rocks and mud. The storms also churn up the water like a washing machine, mixing coastal sediments into it. This can reduce the amount of sunlight that reaches marine habitats. Near human settlements, debris and sewage may continue to flow into the sea long after the storm has passed.

Seagrass meadows—shallow marine water habitats that support creatures such as lobsters, shrimp, conch, and finfish— are particularly vulnerable. Plants are ripped up or buried under sediments. Irma inflicted heavy damage on seagrass near Florida and the Caribbean islands it hit. That could potentially impact not only fisheries but also tourism. Seagrass stabilizes sediments and thus protects the popular white-sand beaches.

The Caribbean marine environment was already suffering from poor water quality and overfishing. Many locations also have

Seagrass meadows, which support rich
ecosystems, can be severely harmed
by hurricanes.

ineffective marine protection laws, which could delay the recovery of the damaged areas. Environmentalists will be keeping a close watch on the marine environment in the years to come as they continue to advocate for more protection.

CHAPTER SEVEN

OTHER
STATES

N ow an immense tropical storm 415 miles (669 km) wide, Irma still carried torrential rain and powerful 70-mile-per-hour (112 kmh) winds as it moved from Florida into Georgia. Georgia's 100-mile (160 km) coastline experienced heavy rain and a storm surge that hit right at high tide. Many communities were swamped for the second time in a year. In early October 2016, Hurricane Matthew had also brought record storm surges and damaging winds and rain to the region.

Falling trees damaged many homes and killed two people. A man was killed when a tree fell on his house, and a woman died when a tree fell on her vehicle. Irma also claimed a third victim in Georgia, a man who had

Though Irma had weakened by the time it reached Georgia, it remained capable of causing widespread flooding and other damage.

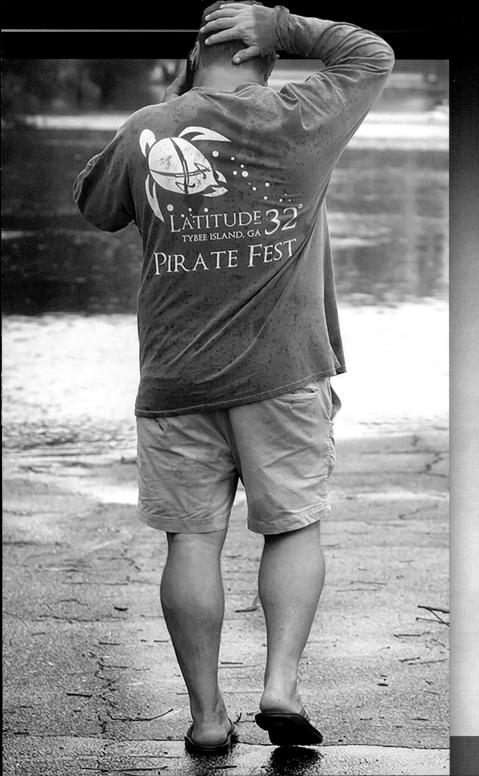

a heart attack while trying to clear debris from his roof at the height of the storm.

Falling trees and branches were among the biggest concerns in Atlanta, which came under its first-ever tropical storm watch. Half of the city's land area is covered by trees, more than in most urban centers. Many of these are huge oak trees. Six crews were kept busy dealing with the tree damage as the storm passed over. When it arrived in Atlanta, the weakening storm brought winds of 45 miles per hour (72 kmh), with gusts up to 64 miles per hour (103 kmh), along with continued heavy rain. Although Hartsfield-Jackson Atlanta International Airport, the nation's busiest, remained open, approximately 800 flights were canceled.[1]

HURRICANE MATTHEW

Just 11 months before Tropical Storm Irma hit Georgia and South Carolina, the area was devastated by Hurricane Matthew. After tearing through the Caribbean, affecting many of the same islands as Irma, the storm caused severe flooding along the US coast as it moved over the ocean east of Florida, Georgia, South Carolina, and North Carolina. It made only one official landfall on the US mainland, coming ashore southeast of McClellanville, South Carolina, on October 8, 2016, as a Category 1 hurricane with 75-mile-per-hour (120 kmh) winds. Overall, Hurricane Matthew was far deadlier than Hurricane Irma. It killed 585 people, including more than 500 in Haiti.[2]

SOUTH CAROLINA

South Carolina also suffered from heavy flooding and high winds, even though the storm's center missed the state. Wind gusts of up to 72 miles per hour (115 kmh) were recorded on Folly Beach. Though Irma's eye was 250 miles (400 km) inland from Charleston, nearly 10 feet (3 m) of water was pushed a mile into the city. That was four feet (1.2 m) above a typical high tide, and it was Charleston's third-highest storm surge on record.[3]

By Monday afternoon, 250,000 people in South Carolina were without power, and flooding and downed trees had closed more than 160 roads in 10 counties. As in other states, much of the damage was caused by falling trees. In Columbia, a massive oak tree fell on a two-story apartment building near the University of South Carolina.

After the hurricane, police patrolled sand-covered streets in South Carolina on all-terrain vehicles.

MORE TO THE
STORY

THE FOLLY BOAT

In 1969, powerful Hurricane Hugo washed a boat from the World War II (1939–1945) era ashore at Folly Beach, South Carolina. It came to rest near a state highway. Over the years, residents painted and repainted messages on it, ranging from marriage proposals to birthday wishes to messages from supporters of rival political candidates and sports teams.

As Tropical Storm Irma approached the area, someone had painted "Godspeed Florida. This too shall pass," in response to the damage to the south. Then came Irma. Folly Beach flooded. Chris John, who owns a dock a short distance away, told CNN a friend of his was looking out the window and said, "Whoa! What is that?"[4]

That turned out to be the Folly Boat, floating atop the rising waters. This was surprising, since the boat was weighted down with cement. John retrieved the floating boat and brought it to his front yard. Whether it will ever make it back to its iconic location by the state highway remains uncertain. Because it left its former resting place, several levels of government permission will be required to put it back.

Luckily, no one was hurt. One fatality in South Carolina was attributed to the storm: a man clearing debris outside his home was killed when he was struck by a falling tree limb.

"WE'RE UNDER WATER. WE HAVE WIRES DOWN, TREES DOWN. VERY LITTLE IS PASSABLE."[6]

— JANE DARBY, MAYOR, EDISTO BEACH, SOUTH CAROLINA

NORTH CAROLINA

Weakening all the time, Tropical Storm Irma was still capable of causing damage as it blew through North Carolina. Some 75,000 people lost power in western counties. Wind gusts of 50 miles per hour (80 kmh) were reported in the mountains.[5] On the coast, several inches of rain fell, causing some minor flooding. A few large trees were toppled in Charlotte, damaging some homes. However, there were no reports of injuries or deaths. Clouds, thunderstorms, rain, and wind would spread through many other states over the next few days as Irma broke apart, but the mighty hurricane that had caused so much death and destruction across the Caribbean and Florida was no more.

CHAPTER EIGHT

THE
AFTERMATH

A s soon as Hurricane Irma had passed, relief and recovery efforts began. But the storm's high winds and flooding had severely damaged many of the roads, harbors, and airports needed for relief to arrive in the devastated areas. On a small, heavily damaged island, there might be few or no resources available locally to help those affected.

This meant that for many of the Caribbean islands hit by Irma, the initial aid came from overseas. The French, British, Dutch, and US militaries all rushed aid to the area. Warships and planes were dispatched with food, water, and troops. For example, the USS *Wasp*, an amphibious warship, was the first US Navy ship to arrive in the US Virgin Islands. It began deploying helicopters

US troops unloaded drinking water in the US Virgin Islands on September 10, 2017.

to assist with damage assessment and deliver supplies. It also carried out medical evacuations of critical-care patients, bringing them from the heavily damaged island of Saint Thomas to the less affected island of Saint Croix. Four additional warships would follow.

A KING AND A PRESIDENT

In some cases, European leaders followed their nations' warships, partially in response to complaints that they had been unprepared and slow to respond to the hurricane. King Willem-Alexander of the Netherlands visited Sint Maarten, the Dutch half of Saint Martin, on Monday, September 11. At the same time, the first evacuees from the island were being reunited with family members in the Netherlands.

French president Emmanuel Macron visited the French side of Saint Martin on September 12. At a press conference on Guadeloupe, also a French territory, he promised that Saint Martin would be "reborn." He pledged €50 million ($60 million) in aid and noted that 2,000 security forces had been sent to the island.[1]

Macron, *center*, met with residents on Saint Martin on September 12.

On September 13, British foreign secretary Boris Johnson visited the British territories of the British Virgin Islands and Anguilla. He pledged £32 million ($43 million) in aid to those islands and the Turks and Caicos, also a British territory. Victor Banks, chief minister of the British overseas territory of Anguilla, said the pledge was "significant," but noted that it wasn't nearly enough. He estimated the cost of repairing the infrastructure on his island alone at £1 billion ($1.4 billion).[2]

SECURITY ISSUES AND SUPPLIES

On many of the affected islands, security became an issue. On Saint Martin, residents who evacuated in the aftermath of the storm said they saw looting and robbery, including a group of people who broke into a high-end resort and robbed guests. "All the food is gone now," Jacques Charbonnier of Saint Martin told the New York Times. "People are fighting in the streets for what is left."[3]

"SOMEONE BROKE INTO OUR HOME AND TRIED TO ROB US, BUT MY PARENTS MANAGED TO SCARE THEM AWAY."[5]

— MAEVA CANAPPELE, 20, RESIDENT OF SAINT MARTIN

In some instances, the security problems delayed the delivery of supplies. Families of those on Saint Martin organized groups of boats from as far away as Guadeloupe. However, several of the arriving ships turned back from the main port because they were afraid of the desperate crowds gathered on the shore.

Some countries that had themselves suffered damage nevertheless offered aid to others. Cuba, though it had its own devastated regions, sent more than 750 health workers to Antigua, Barbuda, Saint Kitts, Nevis, Saint Lucia, the Bahamas, Dominica, and Haiti.[4] Puerto Rico, having been spared the worst damage, became a hub for providing aid to other countries. Puerto Ricans donated water, clothing, and other supplies. Recreational boaters sailed to the nearby islands to deliver the supplies and to evacuate homeless islanders.

WEEKS LATER, SOME IMPROVEMENT

By mid-October, with millions of dollars in aid from governments, the United Nations, and nongovernmental organizations including the Red Cross flowing into the region, things were improving in the Caribbean. However, progress was slow and uneven. The situation was made worse on some islands when Hurricane Maria swept through just two weeks after Irma, adding to the misery and in some cases destroying what little was left. Maria also devastated Puerto Rico, which had been helping its neighbors after emerging from Irma relatively unharmed.

In Barbuda, the evacuation order was lifted, allowing families to start to return. The government brought in workers to repair water and electricity infrastructure. New power lines were to be installed underground to protect them from future storms. The World Bank had approved a $40 million loan for reconstruction of the island, but that was less than half of what Gordon Browne, the prime minister of Antigua and Barbuda, had asked for.

Residents of Barbuda returned to find their homes and neighborhoods torn apart.

He stated at least $100 million would be needed, and he urged business owners and the international community to contribute.[6]

In Anguilla, authorities planned to have the island open for business again by Christmas, although with limited capacity for tourists. Most of the major hotels didn't expect to reopen until sometime in 2018. Phone and Internet access were restored, along with power for most of the island. Roads and beaches were cleared, and restaurants and businesses were reopening. A temporary ferry terminal for use by residents of Anguilla and Saint Martin opened to replace the Blowing Point Ferry Terminal, which had been destroyed by the storm.

THE VIRGIN ISLANDS STILL STRUGGLING

The hard-hit British Virgin Islands were still closed to tourists by mid-October. The major tourist hotels were expected to stay closed for as long as two years. However, smaller resorts were being restored, and the first cruise visitors returned in November, which was when the airports were reopening for commercial traffic as well. The government offered loan programs for small businesses and cost breaks on construction materials to help stimulate the reconstruction process.

The US Virgin Islands were likewise closed for all of October. Saint Thomas and Saint John had suffered the worst damage from Irma, while Saint Croix had largely been spared. Saint Croix was hit by Hurricane Maria, however, leaving all three major islands in much the same condition. By mid-October, curfews were still in effect for residents as authorities worked to restore utilities. The hope was to have services restored to 90 percent of homes and businesses by the holiday season.[7]

FEMA estimated the total volume of debris that had to be cleared from the US Virgin Islands in the wake of two successive hurricanes at 1.1 million cubic yards (841,000 cubic m).[8] Despite the challenges, the US Virgin Islands reopened for cruise ships in November. Some shops and restaurants were reopening, and officials were clearing debris from Virgin Islands National Park.

FAMOUS AIRPORT REOPENS

Access to the entire area was improved when Princess Juliana International Airport on the Dutch side of Saint Martin reopened on October 10. Although many residents were still in need of ongoing assistance, some restaurants and small businesses were reopening. On the Dutch side,

British troops helped residents clear debris from the British Virgin Islands.

70 percent of the hotel rooms had been destroyed, a major blow to an island that relies on tourism for at least 90 percent of its economy. However, room capacity was expected to be up to 50 percent by the end of the year and to continue to recover into 2018.[9]

In the Turks and Caicos, utilities were largely restored on most of the islands by mid-October. Businesses were reopening, and ferries were running. Recovery was slower on the hardest-hit islands—Grand Turk, South Caicos, and Salt Cay. The cruise port on Grand Turk reopened in November.

SLOW RECOVERY IN CUBA

In Cuba, recovery efforts were lagging in the weeks following the storm. Preliminary estimates of the damage there included 158,000 homes damaged, including 14,657 that collapsed entirely and another 23,000 that lost their roofs. Some 235,000 acres (95,000 ha) of crops were destroyed, with so many chicken farms damaged that eggs were rationed throughout the country. By the end of September 2017, 11,689 people were still dependent on the government for basic necessities.[10]

Cuban workers took to the streets of Havana with industrial equipment to clear debris.

Cuba received millions of dollars in aid from the United Nations, the European Union, and countries such as Venezuela, Russia, Panama, Japan, the United Kingdom, and Honduras. All the same, a local newspaper reported that one month after Irma's landfall in Cuba, the northern coastal region of Sancti Spiritus looked as though the hurricane had just hit. Many people were still living in evacuation centers.

RECOVERING FROM "THE IRMANATOR"

The hard-hit Florida Keys, like other Caribbean islands, struggled to restart their tourism industry in the wake of what some residents had started calling "the Irmanator," a play on the killer robots from the Terminator movies. Irma tore a 97-mile (155 km) path of destruction through the Lower Keys. Mountains of debris were piled alongside the Overseas Highway, but bridges were soon reopened, and power was restored in most places.

The region officially reopened for tourism on October 1. Key West and Key Largo, which escaped the brunt of the storm, were largely back to normal by then, but many properties on the Atlantic side of the Keys were expected to be closed for months. One major concern was keeping workers employed. Businesses feared their employees might be forced to move away and would never come back.

Closer to the mainland, Marco Island, where Irma made its second landfall as a Category 3 storm, was all but normal by mid-October—much to the surprise even of some of its residents. On the Sunday night of the storm, the southern part of the island was under one to two feet (30 to 60 cm) of standing water, the most that longtime residents had ever seen. The next morning, uprooted trees, downed power lines, and debris were everywhere.

However, while 15 homes lost roofs, the rest suffered only minimal damage. Even the older houses came through relatively unscathed. Six weeks later, it was nearly impossible to tell a hurricane had ever passed over the island.

SUFFERING IN TRAILER PARKS

On the mainland, however, trailer parks, where the homes were less sturdy, were far from back to normal. Many were badly damaged by the wind and water. One of the hardest-hit towns was Immokalee, where mobile homes

Fragile trailer homes were no match for Irma's powerful gusts.

make up a quarter of the housing and half the population lives in poverty. By the middle of October, 57 families in Collier County, where Immokalee is located, had been approved to receive temporary trailers, but only 10 of these trailers had been delivered.[11] Many other people were still waiting for help.

Throughout Florida, Georgia, and the Carolinas, communities and individuals were still working to clean up their neighborhoods and repair the damage from Irma. As of October 20, for example, Florida governor Rick Scott had authorized $141 million in emergency spending, as well as $25 million in interest-free loans for citrus growers, whose crops were damaged by the storm.[12]

DAMAGE ESTIMATES

By the end of October, more than 750,000 insurance claims worth $5.3 billion had been filed in Florida due to Hurricane Irma. These figures continued to grow. Two-thirds of the claims were from homeowners.[13]

The initial estimate for damage to Florida's agriculture industry was $2.5 billion, with $700 million of that hitting the citrus industry in particular. Because Florida provides

KENNEDY SPACE CENTER WEATHERS IRMA

The center of Irma came within just 65 miles (105 km) of Kennedy Space Center at 2:00 a.m. on September 11. Some facilities suffered roof damage or water leaks. The spaceport had also been damaged by Hurricane Matthew 11 months before. The areas that were repaired after that storm weathered Irma better because they had been built to updated standards.

Kennedy Space Center is home to the massive Vehicle Assembly Building, where Saturn V rockets used for the moon landing missions were assembled. The structure is 526 feet (160 m) tall, and it experienced extremely strong winds. Wind speeds were clocked at 67 to 94 miles per hour (107 to 150 kmh) at 54 feet (17 m) off the ground. Monitors 428 feet (130 m) high measured speeds up to 116 miles per hour (185 kmh).[14]

Irma's sheer size meant it lingered over the site for about four and a half hours, far longer than Hurricane Matthew the previous year. But the spaceport came through in good shape, reopening on September 15. The majority of employees were back at work on September 18, even though many still lacked power or water at home.

about one-half of the nation's orange juice, there were some concerns about higher orange juice prices nationwide. However, major store chains were able to find other suppliers from California and elsewhere, so customers saw little impact.

Hurricanes cost countries not only through the physical damage caused but also through their effects on the economy. In the Caribbean, much of the economy is based on tourism. While the full effects of Irma and the other hurricanes of 2017 were unknown in the storms' immediate aftermath, even a one-percent drop in visitors to the region would cost $138 million directly.

Over time, such a drop could deliver a $214 million hit to the region's GDP.[15]

ECONOMIC COSTS

The actual damage across the Caribbean and into the United States from Hurricane Irma was estimated at $62 billion. However, the Perryman Group, an economic and financial analysis firm, estimated that the economic cost to the United States alone would end up being $76.2 billion in lost gross domestic production, $50.5 billion in lost real personal income, and 553,700 lost person-years of employment.[16]

That effect on employment showed up in US job statistics in September 2017. Approximately 33,000 jobs were lost nationwide that month, the first job loss in seven years. That was largely influenced by the 127,000 jobs lost in Florida because of Irma, mostly in hotels, restaurants, and construction.[17] However, the jobs were expected to bounce back in the coming months as the recovery effort continued.

Calculating the total cost of something like a hurricane is complicated because hurricanes are complicated.

MORE TO THE
STORY

LOSS OF A LANDMARK HOTEL

One victim of Hurricane Irma was one of the oldest resorts on Sint Maarten. Damage to the Summit Hotel Resort, built in the early 1970s, was "catastrophic," owner Bruce Jakubovitz wrote to members of the hotel's vacation club.[18]

Jakubovitz said some of the hotel's buildings were flattened completely, and all but one of the Summit's two-story buildings had their second floors either partially or completely blown off. The single-story buildings lost roofs and suffered other damage. The pool deck was completely blown away. The quarters of the general manager and the head of housekeeping were destroyed. The restaurant, bar, reception office, laundry facilities, and maintenance building were also either destroyed or heavily damaged. Some staff lost their homes in the hurricane, and all were left unemployed. Jakubovitz asked for donations to a fund-raising campaign to help support them.

The hotel opened in 1973 and had survived many previous hurricanes. But Hurricane Irma, with its sustained winds of 185 miles per hour (296 kmh) and gusts of up to 200 miles per hour (320 kmh), put an end to its operations, as it did to many other resorts and businesses.

Costs include physical damage to buildings, vehicles, and boats, plus their contents; losses due to business operations being interrupted; damage to infrastructure such as roads, bridges, and buildings; and damage to crops, livestock, and timber. These costs do not take into account injuries, deaths, or many other ways in which a hurricane causes damage. In

the United States, the National Centers for Environmental Information calculates the cost of natural disasters, but the analysts themselves say, "Our estimates should be considered conservative with respect to what is truly lost, but cannot be completely measured."[19]

Regardless of how it was measured, Irma was a terrifying, catastrophic disaster, one of the strongest hurricanes on record. Just as people do after every disaster, the public started asking why it had been so damaging and what could be done to lessen the damage from similar storms in the future.

CHAPTER NINE

A GLIMPSE OF
THE FUTURE?

T he power and size of Hurricane Irma, as well as the hurricanes that came in the weeks before and after it, caught the world's attention. These storms prompted people to wonder why the 2017 hurricane season was so devastating. In particular, people wondered if blame for the strength and destructiveness of the hurricanes could be laid at the feet of anthropogenic climate change. This process is caused by increasing levels of carbon dioxide and other greenhouse gases in the atmosphere due to humanity's burning of fossil fuels. When greenhouse gases build up in the atmosphere, they trap the sun's heat rather than letting that heat escape into space. The result is a warming average global temperature. Because warmer

Experts in weather and climate are studying Irma and storms like it to determine how hurricanes are affected by climate change.

oceans provide the energy that fuels hurricanes, there seemed to be a possible link between climate change and destructive hurricanes. At the same time, climate change melts the ice caps, and the warming oceans undergo expansion, raising the sea level and increasing the severity of storm surges. Questions about the connections between hurricanes and climate change had also been raised after Hurricane Katrina in 2005, which killed more than 1,800 people in the Caribbean and the United States and devastated the city of New Orleans, Louisiana.[1]

In the years since, the United States has seen much less major hurricane activity. Until Hurricane Harvey, no Category 3 or stronger hurricane had made landfall in the United States since Hurricane Wilma, which struck in the same year as Hurricane Katrina. Other, smaller storms had hit during this period. For example, Hurricane Ike, a Category 2 storm, tore up a large portion of the Texas coastline in 2007. The year 2017, it seemed, more than made up for that, and the climate change questions were immediately raised again.

While some activists were quick to claim the 2017 hurricanes were definitive proof that the changing climate

MORE TO THE
STORY

IRMA FACTS AND FIGURES

Hurricane Irma's maximum sustained winds of 185 miles per hour (296 kmh) tied with the 1935 Florida Keys hurricane, Hurricane Gilbert, and Hurricane Wilma for the second-strongest maximum winds on record in the Atlantic. These storms rank behind 1980's Hurricane Allen, which had winds of up to 190 miles per hour (304 kmh). Irma maintained its maximum for 37 hours, the longest any recorded cyclone anywhere has kept such intensity. It spent 3.25 days as a Category 5 hurricane, tying with a hurricane that struck Cuba in 1932 for the longest lifetime as a Category 5 in the Atlantic.

Irma's lowest recorded central pressure, 914 millibars, was the lowest pressure of an Atlantic hurricane outside the western Caribbean and Gulf of Mexico on record. That record was broken a few weeks later by Hurricane Maria, which reached a central pressure of 908 millibars. Irma generated more energy than the first eight named storms of the 2017 Atlantic hurricane season combined, and as much all by itself as is produced by an entire average Atlantic hurricane season. Finally, Irma was the strongest storm on record to ever hit the Leeward Islands. The previous strongest were the Okeechobee Hurricane of 1928 and Hurricane David of 1979, both of which hit the islands with maximum sustained winds of 160 miles per hour (256 kmh).[2]

was already making storms more powerful, in general the scientific community was more cautious. As the US Climate Science Special Report, prepared for the US government's 2018 National Climate Assessment, notes, determining the role climate change plays in hurricanes is difficult because hurricanes are so rare. That makes it difficult to establish a trend.

The difficulty is increased because it is only since the mid-1960s that satellites have made it possible to accurately track all hurricanes. A comprehensive report on climate change and hurricanes prepared by NOAA points out that a large number of the storms observed since the mid-1960s would not have been observed before that, when the only way a hurricane far out at sea would be detected was if a ship or airplane happened to encounter it. After estimating the number of missing storms in the historical record, the report found that the slight positive trend in storm occurrence from 1878 to 2006 was statistically insignificant. And of course, if some storms were missed in the past, then researchers don't have a record of their intensity either. Still, researchers have used computer climate models to show that as the climate

It is difficult to link an individual storm directly to climate change, but broader trends in storm intensity are predicted to emerge over time.

warms, hurricanes are expected to become more intense, and their intensification is expected to happen more rapidly than in the past.

THE HUMAN IMPACT

The Fifth Assessment Report of the United Nations Intergovernmental Panel on Climate Change (IPCC), released in 2014, expressed "low confidence" of a human contribution to the changes in tropical cyclone activity since 1950. It extended that "low confidence" to the likelihood of changes in the early twenty-first century. However, it stated that by the late twenty-first century, it was "more likely than not" that human-caused changes in the western North Pacific and North Atlantic will be detected.[3]

The NOAA report agreed: "It is premature to conclude that human activities—and particularly greenhouse gas emissions that cause global warming—have already had a detectable impact on Atlantic hurricane or global tropical cyclone activity."[4] However, the report adds that humans might have caused changes that are not yet detectable, and it notes that by the end of this century, human-caused global warming is likely to intensify tropical cyclones around the world, producing higher rainfall rates and more destructive potential. So while it may be premature to say Irma was directly caused or made stronger by climate change, its strength and the damage it caused could be a preview of what to expect in the coming decades.

PLANNING FOR THE FUTURE

Many experts agree that countries in hurricane-affected regions need to take these projections into account in their future planning. The *Economist* magazine charged in an editorial that governments in the Caribbean have so far failed to do the "hard things" they need to do to make the islands more resistant to hurricane damage. Although building codes are often rewritten after a storm hits, they haven't been well enforced, the magazine points out. As a result, too much of the population lives in houses that aren't strong enough to withstand major storms. Protective natural features such as mangrove swamps have been ripped out by developers so they can put hotels on beaches. Politicians concerned more about getting elected than about the long-term safety of their islands have a hard time making the difficult decisions required.

According to the *Economist*, billions of dollars need to be spent in the Caribbean on upgrading buildings, as well as roads and other infrastructure. Burying new power lines on Barbuda and other islands after Irma is one example of such an upgrade. As islands rebuild, they should ensure housing, hotels, and roads are built farther from the shore and to higher standards. The Caribbean countries should also work more closely together to enable fleets of boats and planes to

"IT'S THIS CONTINUED DEVELOPMENT IN VULNERABLE AREAS THAT'S INCREASING OUR HURRICANE RISK MUCH MORE THAN CLIMATE CHANGE ITSELF."[5]

— DAVID ZIERDEN, FLORIDA'S STATE CLIMATOLOGIST

be mobilized on short notice to help devastated islands, and they should ensure their joint disaster-response organizations are well funded.

The magazine concludes, however, that better planning and more cooperation won't be enough: "Caribbean islands will need help from their European and North American patrons and other donors to adapt to the disasters that will follow Irma. And global action on climate must become much more ambitious. Otherwise, large parts of paradise will eventually be washed away."[6] All of that will take time, political will, negotiations, and money. Meanwhile, the hurricanes will keep coming. Hurricane Irma was a record-breaking storm in terms of its strength and destructiveness. It may also be remembered for spurring difficult conversations about why powerful hurricanes are forming and what can be done to limit their devastation in the future.

The Caribbean will always be vulnerable to hurricanes. It will be up to policymakers to determine how the region prepares for and responds to these deadly storms.

ESSENTIAL
FACTS

MAJOR EVENTS

- On August 27, 2017, Hurricane Irma is born from a wave of low pressure that emerges from the western African coast.

- On September 5, Irma makes landfall on the small island of Barbuda, devastating it with winds of up to 185 mph (296 kmh), making it the strongest storm to ever hit the Leeward Islands.

- Irma makes landfall in the Florida Keys on September 10 as a Category 4 storm, then hits the mainland later that day as a Category 3.

- On September 11, Irma hits southern Georgia as a tropical storm, doing considerable damage there and in the Carolinas. Its last remnants pass out to sea on September 15.

KEY PLAYERS

- The Federal Emergency Management Agency (FEMA) coordinated the US government response to the storm in the US Virgin Islands and the US mainland.

- The National Hurricane Center, a division of the National Oceanic and Atmospheric Administration, tracked the hurricane from start to finish and provided forecasts that helped guide storm preparations and evacuation.

IMPACT ON SOCIETY

The final death toll was estimated at 134, with damage estimated at between $50 billion and $100 billion. In the months after the storm, some of the less damaged Caribbean islands were showing signs of recovery. Tourists and cruise ships were returning. However, the hardest hit areas remained closed, as work continued to restore power and other basic services. Complete recovery was expected to take months or years.

QUOTE

"These storms know no borders—they cross them at will and with no fear of being turned away. . . . They make no discrimination between small or large, or poor or rich. They see no white people, or black people, or any shade of colour in between. Their destruction is ruthless, heartless, and pitiless."

—Sir Ronald Sanders, Antigua and Barbuda ambassador to the United States

GLOSSARY

ANTHROPOGENIC
Caused or produced by humans.

CARBON DIOXIDE
A gas with the chemical formula of CO_2 that is released when people breathe and when fossil fuels are burned.

EVACUATION
The removal of people from an area for reasons of safety.

EYEWALL
A wall of clouds surrounding the eye of a hurricane; the eyewall contains the most damaging winds and intense rainfall.

FORECAST CONE

The projected possible path of a hurricane.

GDP

Gross domestic product, the monetary value of all goods and services produced within a nation's geographic borders over a specified period of time.

LANDFALL

The event of a storm moving over land after it has been over water.

STORM SURGE

An abnormal rise in sea level during a storm, measured by how much higher it is than the normal level at whatever stage the tide is at.

TROPICAL DEPRESSION

A low pressure area accompanied by thunderstorms that produce a circular wind flow with maximum sustained winds below 39 mph (62 kmh).

TROPICAL STORM

A large spinning storm system with winds at or above 39 miles per hour (62 kmh) and no higher than 73 miles per hour (118 kmh).

ADDITIONAL
RESOURCES

SELECTED BIBLIOGRAPHY

Collins, J. M., R. Rohli, and C. Paxton. *Florida Weather and Climate: More than Just Sunshine.* Gainesville, FL: UP of Florida, 2017. Print.

Collins, Jennifer, and Paul Flaherty. "Keeping an 'Eye' on Tropical Research Data." *Florida Geographer* 45 (2014): 14–27. Print.

"Detailed Meteorological Summary on Hurricane Irma." *National Weather Service.* NWS, 2017. Web. 31 Oct. 2017.

FURTHER READINGS

Brown, Don. *Drowned City: Hurricane Katrina and New Orleans.* Boston, MA: HMH, 2017. Print.

Challoner, Jack. *Eyewitness Hurricane & Tornado.* New York: DK, 2014. Print.

Waterford, Cliff. *Hurricane Harvey.* Minneapolis, MN: Abdo, 2018. Print.

ONLINE RESOURCES

Booklinks
NONFICTION NETWORK
FREE! ONLINE NONFICTION RESOURCES

To learn more about Hurricane Irma, visit **abdobooklinks.com**. These links are routinely monitored and updated to provide the most current information available.

MORE INFORMATION

For more information on this subject, contact or visit the following organizations:

Federal Emergency Management Agency (FEMA)
500 C Street SW
Washington, DC 20472
202-646-2500
fema.gov
FEMA's mission is to support citizens and first responders to ensure they can work together to build, sustain, and improve the nation's capability to prepare for and recover from disasters.

National Oceanic and Atmospheric Administration
National Hurricane Center
11691 SW 17th Street
Miami, FL 33165
305-229-4404
nhc.noaa.gov
The National Hurricane Center's mission is to save lives and reduce property loss by issuing watches, warnings, forecasts, and analyses of hazardous tropical weather.

SOURCE
NOTES

CHAPTER 1. A TASTE OF THINGS TO COME

1. Tara John. "'There Is No Home to Go Back To.' Hurricane Irma Flattens Barbuda, Leaving a Population Stranded." *Time*. Time, 11 Sept. 2017. Web. 20 Dec. 2017.

2. "What Is a Hurricane?" *National Ocean Service*. NOAA, 10 Oct. 2017. Web. 20 Dec. 2017.

3. Ann M. Simmons. "Once There Was an Island known as Barbuda. After Hurricane Irma, Much of It Is Gone." *LA Times*. LA Times, 7 Sept. 2017. Web. 20 Dec. 2017.

4. "Antigua and Barbuda." *World Factbook*. CIA, 12 Dec. 2017. Web. 20 Dec. 2017.

5. Joe Sterling and Cassandra Santiago. "For First Time in 300 Years, No One Is Living on Barbuda." *CNN*. CNN, 15 Sept. 2017. Web. 20 Dec. 2017.

6. Natalie Musumeci. "Toddler Ripped from Caregiver's Arms Among Irma's Dead." *New York Post*. New York Post, 8 Sept. 2017. Web. 20 Dec. 2017.

7. Alexa Maines. "2017 Atlantic Hurricane Season By The Numbers: An Extremely Active Season." *WeatherBug*. WeatherBug, 29 Dec. 2017. Web. 29 Dec. 2017.

8. Tara John. "These Are the Islands Hit by Hurricane Irma." *Time*. Time, 8 Sept. 2017. Web. 20 Dec. 2017.

CHAPTER 2. A HURRICANE IS BORN

1. Sir Ronald Sanders. "Lessons from Hurricane Irma." *Jamaica Observer*. Jamaica Observer, 17 Sept. 2017. Web. 20 Dec. 2017.

2. Phil Stewart. "Exclusive: Flying into the Eye of Hurricane Irma with US 'Hurricane Hunters.'" *Reuters*. Reuters, 9 Sept. 2017. Web. 20 Dec. 2017.

CHAPTER 3. GETTING READY IN THE CARIBBEAN

1. "Advisory Number 10." *National Hurricane Center*. NOAA, 1 Sept. 2017. Web. 20 Dec. 2017.

2. "Advisory Number 17." *National Hurricane Center*. NOAA, 3 Sept. 2017. Web. 20 Dec. 2017.

3. Allie Capron. "Hurricane Irma Doesn't Have to Be a Disaster Says TCI's Disaster Management Director." *Turks & Caicos Sun*. Turks & Caicos Sun, 5 Sept. 2017. Web. 20 Dec. 2017.

4. Travis Cartwright-Carroll. "Government to Provide for Mandatory Evacuations." *Nassau Guardian*. Nassau Guardian, 11 Sept. 2017. Web. 20 Dec 2017.

5. "Jamaica Trying to Determine Severity of Irma's Impact on Caribbean Neighbors." *Jamaica Observer*. Jamaica Observer, 8 Sept. 2017. Web. 20 Dec. 2017.

6. "Hurricane Irma Wreaks Apocalyptic Damage in the Caribbean." *Washington Post*. New Orleans Times-Picayune, 7 Sept. 2017. Web. 20 Dec. 2017.

7. Michael Greshko. "Why This Hurricane Season Has Been So Catastrophic." *National Geographic*. National Geographic, 22 Sept. 2017. Web. 20 Dec. 2017.

8. Mimi Whitefield. "Hurricane Warnings in Effect for Cuba's North Central Coast." *Miami Herald*. Miami Herald, 7 Sept. 2017. Web. 20 Dec. 2017.

CHAPTER 4. PREPARATIONS IN FLORIDA

1. Giovanna Maselli. "Florida Governor Declares State Of Emergency Over Hurricane Irma." *CBS Miami.* CBS, 4 Sept. 2017. Web. 20 Dec. 2017.

2. "Governor Scott Activates 4,000 National Guard Members, 7,000 to Report for Duty Friday Morning." *WFTS Tampa Bay.* ABC, 5 Sept. 2017. Web. 20 Dec. 2017.

3. Josh Delk. "Nearly 7 Million Asked to Evacuate Ahead of Hurricane Irma." *Hill.* Hill, 9 Sept. 2017. Web. 20 Dec. 2017.

4. Ralph Ellis and Eric Levenson. "Floridians Jam Highways to Flee Hurricane Irma." *CNN.* CNN, 7 Sept. 2017. Web. 20 Dec. 2017.

5. Robert Ferris. "Hurricane Irma Downgraded to Category 2 Storm with 100 mph Winds." *CNBC.* CNBC, 10 Sept. 2017. Web. 20 Dec. 2017.

6. Ralph Ellis and Eric Levenson. "Floridians Jam Highways to Flee Hurricane Irma." *CNN.* CNN, 7 Sept. 2017. Web. 20 Dec. 2017.

7. Lizette Alvarez and Marc Santora. "Hurricane Irma Barrels Toward US, Threatening to Engulf Florida." *New York Times.* New York Times, 8 Sept. 2017. Web. 20 Dec. 2017.

8. Ibid.

9. Kristina Torres. "Hurricane Irma: Georgia Governor Nathan Deal Extends State of Emergency to 64 More Counties." *Atlanta Journal-Constitution.* Atlanta Journal-Constitution, 8 Sept. 2017. Web. 20 Dec. 2017.

CHAPTER 5. IRMA HITS THE ISLANDS

1. Gemma Handy. "What It's Like in Barbuda, the Island Ripped Apart by Irma and Forgotten by the World." *Independent.* Independent, 11 Sept. 2017. Web. 20 Dec. 2017.

2. Blair Shiff and Aaron Katersky. "Hurricane Irma Hit Barbuda Like a 'Bomb,' Prime Minister Says." *ABC News.* ABC News, 7 Sept. 2017. Web. 20 Dec. 2017.

3. Ibid.

4. "Saint Martin." *World Factbook.* CIA, 27 Oct. 2017. Web. 20 Dec. 2017.

5. Claire Phipps. "Irma's Destruction: Island by Island." *Guardian.* Guardian, 10 Sept. 2017. Web. 20 Dec. 2017.

6. "In Hurricane's Irma's Ruinous Wake: 'I Feel Like I'm on the Moon.'" *New York Times.* New York Times, 7 Sept. 2017. Web. 20 Dec. 2017.

7. Tara John. "These Are the Islands Hit by Hurricane Irma." *Time.* Time, 8 Sept. 2017. Web. 20 Dec. 2017.

8. Robinson Meyer. "Hurricane Irma: 'Everything Is Under Water, I Mean Everything.'" *Atlantic.* Atlantic, 10 Sept. 2017. Web. 20 Dec. 2017.

9. Claire Phipps. "Irma's Destruction: Island by Island." *Guardian.* Guardian, 10 Sept. 2017. Web. 20 Dec. 2017.

10. Hayley Miller. "These Caribbean Islands Are Reeling after Hurricane Irma's Deadly Damage." *Huffington Post.* Huffington Post, 12 Sept. 2017. Web. 20 Dec. 2017.

11. Eliza Mackintosh and Donie O'Sullivan. "Don't Forget about Us: Irma's Desperate Caribbean Survivors." *CNN.* CNN, 11 Sept. 2017. Web. 20 Dec. 2017.

12. Claire Phipps. "Irma's Destruction: Island by Island." *Guardian.* Guardian, 10 Sept. 2017. Web. 20 Dec. 2017.

13. Ibid.

14. Luis Ferré-Sadurní. "Irma Grazes Puerto Rico but Lays Bare an Infrastructure Problem." *New York Times.* New York Times, 10 Sept. 2017. Web. 20 Dec. 2017.

15. Claire Phipps. "Irma's Destruction: Island by Island." *Guardian.* Guardian, 10 Sept. 2017. Web. 20 Dec. 2017.

16. Travis Cartwright-Carrol. "Ragged Island in the Bahamas Declared Uninhabitable after Hurricane Irma." *Nassau Guardian.* Nassau Guardian, 13 Sept. 2017. Web. 20 Dec. 2017.

17. Sloan Smith. "Bahamians in TCI Recall Irma Nightmare." *Nassau Guardian.* Nassau Guardian, 12 Sept. 2017. Web. 20 Dec. 2017.

18. Patrick Oppmann. "Cuba's old buildings Were no Match for Hurricane Irma." *CNN.* CNN, 15 Sept. 2017. Web. 20 Dec. 2017.

19. Jon Lee Anderson. "Cuba and the Hurricanes of the Caribbean." *New Yorker.* New Yorker, 19 Sept. 2017. Web. 20 Dec. 2017.

20. Laura Smith-Spark and Patrick Oppmann. "Cuba Blasted as Hurricane Irma Tears through the Caribbean." *CNN.* CNN, 9 Sept. 2017. Web. 20 Dec. 2017.

SOURCE NOTES
CONTINUED

CHAPTER 6. LANDFALL IN FLORIDA

1. Robinson Meyer. "Hurricane Irma: 'Everything Is Under Water, I Mean Everything.'" *Atlantic*. Atlantic, 10 Sept. 2017. Web. 20 Dec. 2017.

2. Max Jaeger. "Florida Keys in Crisis as State Cleans up after Irma." *New York Post*. New York Post, 11 Sept. 2017. Web. 20 Dec. 2017.

3. Nick Allen, Rob Crilly, David Millward, Danny Boyle, and Chris Graham. "Hurricane Irma: Florida Begins the Big Clean Up after Storm Battering as Death Toll Continues to Rise." *Telegraph*. Telegraph, 12 Sept. 2017. Web. 20 Dec. 2017.

4. Pam Wright. "Herd of 949 Endangered Florida Key Deer Survived Irma's Landfall, Wildlife Officials Say." *Weather Channel*. Weather Channel, 23 Oct. 2017. Web. 20 Dec. 2017.

5. Robinson Meyer. "Hurricane Irma: 'Everything Is Under Water, I Mean Everything.'" *Atlantic*. Atlantic, 10 Sept. 2017. Web. 20 Dec. 2017.

6. Jennifer Chu. "'Grey Swan' Cyclones Predicted to be More Frequent and Intense." *MIT News*. MIT, 31 Aug. 2015. Web. 20 Dec. 2017.

7. "Irma Leaves 6.2 Million Florida Homes in the Dark—Over 60% of the Entire States." *CNBC*. CNBC, 11 Sept. 2017. Web. 20 Dec. 2017.

8. "Jacksonville Sees Record-Setting Flooding in Wake of Irma." *CBS News*. CBS, 11 Sept. 2017. Web. 20 Dec. 2017.

9. "Irma Leaves 6.2 Million Florida Homes in the Dark—Over 60% of the Entire States." *CNBC*. CNBC, 11 Sept. 2017. Web. 20 Dec. 2017.

10. Gal Tziperman Lotan. "Hurricane Irma: Deadly Storm Knocks Out Power to More Than 4 Million Customers." *Orlando Sentinel*. Orlando Sentinel, 11 Sept. 2017. Web. 20 Dec. 2017.

11. Andrew Viglucci, Carli Teproff, and Daniel Chang. "Irma Could Have Been a Lot Worse for South Florida, But It's Still Not a Pretty Picture." *Miami Herald*. Miami Herald, 11 Sept. 2017. Web. 20 Dec. 2017.

12. Dan Scanlan. "Weeks after Irma, Florida Is Still Counting the Dead." *Florida Times-Union*. Florida Times-Union, 7 Oct. 2017. Web. 20 Dec. 2017.

CHAPTER 7. OTHER STATES

1. "Irma Whips Southeast: 3 Dead in Georgia, 1 in South Carolina." *MSN*. MSN, 11 Sept. 2017. Web. 20 Dec. 2017.

2. "World Meteorological Organization Retires Storm Names Matthew and Otto." *NOAA*. NOAA, 27 Mar. 2017. Web. 20 Dec. 2017.

3. "Irma Causes Severe Flooding, Power Outages in South Carolina." *CBS News*. CBS News, 11 Sept. 2017. Web. 20 Dec. 2017.

4. Doug Criss. "Hurricane Irma Washes Away Iconic Boat—28 years after Hurricane Hugo Washed It Ashore." *CNN*. CNN, 12 Sept. 2017. Web. 20 Dec. 2017.

5. "About 4,500 Without Power after Irma Blows Through Parts of NC." *WRAL*. WRAL, 12 Sept. 2017. Web. 20 Dec. 2017.

6. "Irma Causes Severe Flooding, Power Outages in South Carolina." *CBS News*. CBS News, 11 Sept. 2017. Web. 20 Dec. 2017.

CHAPTER 8. THE AFTERMATH

1. "Emmanuel Macron Pledges €50m to Help Irma-ravaged Caribbean Territories." *Guardian*. Guardian, 12 Sept. 2017. Web. 20 Dec. 2017.

2. Samuel Osborne. "Boris Johnson Witnesses Hurricane Irma Devastation on Visit to Anguilla in Caribbean." *Independent*. Independent, 13 Sept. 2017. Web. 20 Dec. 2017.

3. Azam Ahmed and Kirk Semple. "Desperation Mounts in Caribbean Islands: 'All the Food Is Gone.'" *New York Times*. New York Times, 10 Sept. 2017. Web. 20 Dec. 2017.

4. Shehab Khan. "Irma: Cuba Sends Hundreds of Doctors to Caribbean Islands Devastated by Hurricane." *Independent*. Independent, 9 Sept. 2017. Web. 20 Dec. 2017.

5. Azam Ahmed and Kirk Semple. "Desperation Mounts in Caribbean Islands: 'All the Food Is Gone.'" *New York Times*. New York Times, 10 Sept. 2017. Web. 20 Dec. 2017.

6. "Antigua and Barbuda Says Reconstruction Loans Unrealistic." *teleSUR TV*. teleSUR TV, 18 Oct. 2017. Web. 20 Dec. 2017.

7. Bailey Freeman. "Caribbean Travel after Irma and Maria: Essential Information." *Lonely Planet*. Lonely Planet, 25 Oct. 2017. Web. 20 Dec. 2017.

8. Ibid.

9. Ibid.

10. Nora Gámez Torres. "Official Press in Central Cuba: Region Looks 'As Though the Hurricane Had Just Hit.'" *Miami Herald*. Miami Herald, 19 Oct. 2017. Web. 20 Dec. 2017.

11. Maria Perez and Greg Stanley. "Paradise Coast Not All Clear; Some Near Naples Still Struggling after Irma." *Naples Daily News*. Naples Daily News, 20 Oct. 2017. Web. 20 Dec. 2017.

12. Nichole Osinski. "Sen. Hukill: Hurricane Irma Aftermath Means New Bills Filed." *Port Orange Observer*. Port Orange Observer, 20 Oct. 2017. Web. 20 Dec. 2017.

13. "Irma Insurance Claims Continue Increasing." *News Service of Florida*. Florida Politics, 24 Oct. 2017. Web. 20 Dec. 2017.

14. Anna Helney. "Kennedy Space Center Safely Weathers Hurricane Irma." *Kennedy Space Center*. NASA, 25 Sept. 2017. Web. 20 Dec. 2017.

15. Jill Disis. "Caribbean Tourism Faces Long Road to Recovery." *Baltimore Times*. Baltimore Times, 23 Oct. 2017. Web. 20 Dec. 2017.

16. "Hurricane Irma to Cost the US Economy an Estimated $76 Billion in Output, Bringing to Total Losses from Hurricanes Harvey and Irma to More Than $227 Billion in Real Gross Domestic Product." *Perryman Group*. Perryman Group, 25 Oct. 2017. Web. 20 Dec. 2017.

17. Christopher Rugaber. "Hurricane Irma Cost Florida 127K jobs, but Most Will Return." *National Post*. Associated Press, 20 Oct. 2017. Web. 20 Dec. 2017.

18. "Summit Resort Hotel Closed after 40+ Years Due to Hurricane Irma Sustained Damages." *Soualiga NewsDay*. Soualiga NewsDay, 24 Oct. 2017. Web. 20 Dec. 2017.

19. "Calculating the Cost of Weather and Climate Disasters." *National Centers for Environmental Information*. NCWI, 25 Oct. 2017. Web. 20 Dec. 2017.

20. "'It's Devastating.' Returning Florida Evacuees Stunned by Extent of Damage from Hurricane Irma." *Fortune*. Reuters, 13 Sept. 2017. Web. 20 Dec. 2017.

CHAPTER 9. A GLIMPSE OF THE FUTURE?

1. "Hurricane Katrina Statistics Fast Facts." *CNN*. CNN, 28 Aug. 2017. Web. 20 Dec. 2017.

2. "Hurricane Irma Meteorological Records/Notable Facts Recap." *Colorado State University Tropical Meteorology Project*. Colorado State University, n.d. Web. 20 Dec. 2017

3. "Table SPM.1. Summary for Policymakers." *United Nations Intergovernmental Panel on Climate Change Fifth Assessment Report*. United Nations, n.d. Web. 20 Dec. 2017.

4. "Global Warming and Hurricanes." *Geophysical Fluid Dynamics Laboratory*. NOAA, 30 Aug. 2017. Web. 20 Dec. 2017.

5. Umair Irfan. "The Stunning Price Tags for Hurricanes Harvey and Irma, Explained." *Vox*. Vox, 18 Sept. 2017. Web. 20 Dec. 2017.

6. "How the Caribbean Should Cope with Hurricane Irma." *Economist*. Economist, 14 Sept. 2017. Web. 20 Dec. 2017.

INDEX

ABOUT THE
AUTHOR

Edward Willett is the author of more than 60 books of fiction and nonfiction for all ages. Born in New Mexico, he grew up in Saskatchewan, Canada. A former journalist, he's also a professional actor and singer. He lives in Regina, Saskatchewan, with his wife, Margaret Anne Hodges, teenaged daughter, Alice, and black Siberian cat, Shadowpaw.